The Scientist's
Guide to Physics™

Discovering

Atoms

MARGARET CHRISTINE CAMPBELL
AND NATALIE GOLDSTEIN

ROSEN
PUBLISHING®

New York

Published in 2012 by The Rosen Publishing Group, Inc.
29 East 21st Street, New York, NY 10010

First Edition

Library of Congress Cataloging-in-Publication Data

Campbell, Margaret Christine.
Discovering atoms / Margaret Christine Campbell, Natalie Goldstein.—1st ed.
     p. cm.—(The scientist's guide to physics)
Includes bibliographical references and index.
ISBN 978-1-4488-4700-6 (lib. bdg.)
1. Atoms—Juvenile literature. 2. Atomic structure—Juvenile literature. 3. Matter—Constitution—Juvenile literature. I. Goldstein, Natalie. II. Title.
QC173.16.C36 2012
539.7—dc22
                                                    2010048416

Manufactured in the United States of America

CPSIA Compliance Information: Batch #S11YA: For further information, contact Rosen Publishing, New York, New York, at 1-800-237-9932.

Contents

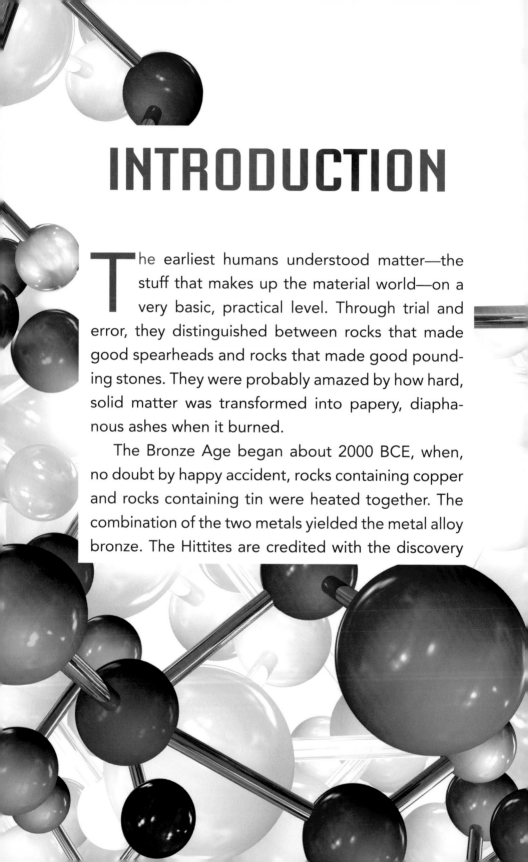

INTRODUCTION

The earliest humans understood matter—the stuff that makes up the material world—on a very basic, practical level. Through trial and error, they distinguished between rocks that made good spearheads and rocks that made good pounding stones. They were probably amazed by how hard, solid matter was transformed into papery, diaphanous ashes when it burned.

The Bronze Age began about 2000 BCE, when, no doubt by happy accident, rocks containing copper and rocks containing tin were heated together. The combination of the two metals yielded the metal alloy bronze. The Hittites are credited with the discovery of iron around 1500 BCE. Metals played a significant role in the growth of chemical knowledge. This is because it was necessary to learn how to separate valued metals from their ores. In addition, as gold and silver coins began to be used for money, it was important to learn how to determine if metals were pure and of the proper weight.

By 4000 BCE, Egyptians were heating combinations of sand, limestone, and soda (sodium carbonate) until the materials melted and turned into glass. The characteristics of glass are quite different from those of the materials used to make it. What was happening to the individual material objects when they were mixed together and underwent such a dramatic transformation and became a different substance?

These questions would lead generations of the world's greatest thinkers, philosophers, and scientists on a long and fascinating quest to discover exactly what was the most basic building block of matter, of the entire physical world. Each generation's questions and best guesses helped increase the collective store of knowledge and push humanity forward to a greater understanding of the material world, how it was formed, and how it worked.

What they were all groping toward was the discovery of the most basic unit of all matter—the atom and the subatomic particles that form its structure.

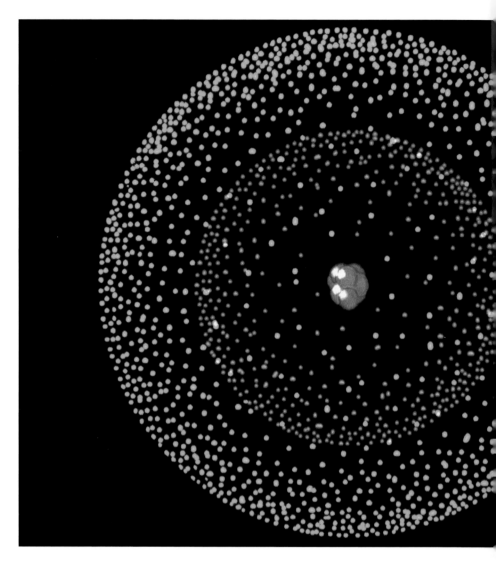

From the theory of the four elements to the alchemists' attempts to discover the philosopher's stone and transform lead into gold, to the early conception of the atom as a sort of microscopic solar system, these early investigations were all flawed and

This computer-generated image depicts an atom of the element beryllium. Its nucleus contains four protons and five neutrons and is surrounded by electron shells (pictured as purple and blue).

ultimately rejected. Yet they also lay the foundation for and made possible the theoretical, technological, and experimental breakthroughs that inform our modern and far more accurate, though by no means yet complete, understanding of the atom, its composition, and its mechanics. This is a rich and fascinating story, full of bizarre theories, false starts, dead ends, and inspiring intellectual insight and vision. In discovering and mapping the atom, scientists have discovered the universe entire.

ANCIENT THEORIES OF MATTER

Chapter

1

Questions regarding natural phenomena and the physical world intrigued the ancient Greeks. Their greatest philosophers tackled the question of the nature of matter. Thales of Miletus, who lived around 600 BCE, stated that all material things are aspects of one fundamental substance—water. He suggested that the amount of water in a substance gave it its unique characteristics.

Another Greek philosopher, Anaximenes, took exception to Thales' argument, insisting that air was the fundamental material. Yet another philosopher suggested that fire was the primary material. A century later, Empedocles of Sicily asked, "Why must there be just one basic substance?" He felt such a conception of matter was too simple. Rather, Empedocles believed that water, air, fire, and earth were the four fundamental "elements," or building blocks, of matter.

The First Atomic Theory

Democritus (ca. 460–370 BCE) was a Greek philosopher who built upon the ideas of his teacher, Leucippus. Democritus said that matter is made up of solid "atoms" and empty space. Materials could be broken apart because of the spaces that exist between the atoms that compose the materials. If matter continues to be divided into smaller and smaller pieces, Democritus reasoned, one would eventually reach a point where the remaining material could no longer be divided.

At this point, the remaining solid and miniscule particle would be "indivisible," or *atomos* in Greek. "Atoms" were indivisible, Democritus said, because they contained no remaining empty space. They were the smallest pieces of substances that existed. They were not only solid, but they were invisible to the naked eye. And they were all alike, that is, atoms were all made from the same fundamental substance, regardless of whether they had been obtained from rock, wood, leaves, or flesh. What made various materials

different from each other was the shape of their atoms or the way those atoms were packed together.

Aristotle's Dead End

The great Greek philosopher Aristotle (384–322 BCE) did not accept Democritus's atomic theory. Aristotle preferred Empedocles' theory of the four elements. He suggested that each of these elements was a combination of two of four opposites—hot and cold, and wet and dry (wet and dry could also refer to soft and hard, respectively). He discussed the properties of substances in terms of their elemental composition— their combinations of water, air, fire, and/or earth—and how they could be transformed by their reaction to their opposites. For example, Aristotle believed that water evaporates when heated because it goes from cold and wet to hot and wet, thereby becoming air. Aristotle actually also added a fifth element known as aether, the divine substance that forms the heavenly spheres and bodies (stars and planets).

The Greek philosopher Democritus is depicted in this portrait from 1652–1653, painted by the Italian artist Luca Giordano. Democritus was the first to suggest that all matter was composed of atoms.

ALCHEMY THROUGH THE AGES AND AROUND THE WORLD

Though long associated in the Western world with medieval Europe, alchemy was a philosophy and proto-scientific practice common to ancient Egypt, Mesopotamia, Babylonia, Persia, India, China, Japan, Korea, Greece, and Rome. The alchemists' two main goals were the transformation of common metals into gold and the discovery of an elixir that would provide eternal life. These seemingly disparate goals were two sides of the same coin, in that the transmutation of lead into gold or silver could be seen as a sort of analogy for the transformation of the frail, base human body into an immortal being (known as "internal alchemy").

At its core, alchemy was an attempt to understand, deconstruct, and reconstruct matter. Its theories and practices seem to have their origin in ancient Egypt about 5000 BCE. The efforts of alchemists through the centuries are credited with advances in ore testing and refining; metalworking; the production of gunpowder, ink, dyes, paints, and cosmetics; glass and ceramic-making; the identification, classification, and use of many substances; and the development of scientific procedures and laboratory equipment.

Asian alchemists tended to place more emphasis on the discovery of useful medicines, while European alchemists were more focused on finding ways to transmute lead into gold. Islamic alchemists worked toward both of these goals, as well as the artificial creation of life. In medieval Europe, alchemists began to gain a bad reputation, often being viewed as counterfeiters, thieves, and cheats. In some countries, the practice of alchemy became banned.

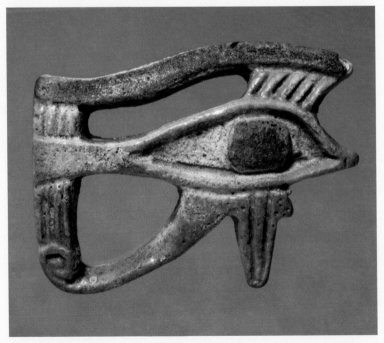

The efforts of alchemists furthered the understanding and practice of metalwork, glasswork, and ceramics. This ancient Egyptian glazed ceramic amulet, composed of quartz and glass, could not have been crafted if not for the experimental breakthroughs of alchemists.

Aristotle is generally regarded as the greatest thinker of his age. Yet many historians believe that Aristotle's dismissal of "atomism" is the main reason scientific inquiry into the nature of matter was stalled for nearly 1,500 years after his death. His influence was so great and he was so highly regarded that few natural philosophers and scientists believed it would be worthwhile to pursue the theory of the atom. If Aristotle rejected this theory, they reasoned, it must be invalid.

ALCHEMISTS AND THE EMERGING FIELD OF CHEMISTRY

Alchemy was the attempt to transmute, or change, one substance into another. It was a direct outgrowth of Aristotle's concept of the transmutability of elements. Alchemists called the agent of transformation the "philosopher's stone," a mysterious chemical preparation that they believed could alter the nature of substances. Alchemists toiled mightily to concoct this miraculous material, using substances such as powder ground from stones and various acids. They believed that when brought into contact with the philosopher's stone, base metals, especially lead,

A medieval-era alchemist studies in his laboratory in this seventeenth-century Dutch painting. He is surrounded by instruments, books, and other objects that indicate mysterious and occult knowledge.

could be transformed into gold. They also believed the philosopher's stone would help them create an elixir that would provide eternal youth and a cure for all human diseases.

Though their theories and practices may seem crude and superstitious, even fantastical, today, most alchemists were learned men and women. In the course of searching for the ever-elusive philosopher's stone, they made some genuinely important contributions to the development of chemistry. Alchemists tested the properties of nearly every substance they could get their hands on. They did not use today's accepted scientific methods, but they did set up laboratories in which they studied some simple chemical processes such as crystallization and distillation. Experiments of a sort were planned and carried out, and detailed records of the results were often kept. The alchemists discovered at least five true elements: arsenic, bismuth, zinc, phosphorus, and antimony. They are also credited with the discovery and description of many chemicals used in their experiments, including nitric acid, acetic acid, and ammonium chloride.

MOVING BEYOND ALCHEMY TOWARD CHEMISTRY

Chapter 2

For centuries, alchemy dominated studies of matter. No less a revered scientific figure than Isaac Newton (1642–1727) is said to have spent a considerable amount of time studying alchemy books. He kept notebooks in which he handcopied the writings of leading alchemists stretching back over a thousand years. He believed that many of these alchemists had written in a sort of riddling code, and he enjoyed trying to solve their puzzles. But he also believed the writings contained genuine secret wisdom that provided the key to understanding the entire universe. But other scientists who

J. Coqman   sculp.

THE HON.^{BLE} ROBERT BOYLE

London Publish'd as the Act directs April 19th 1800 by J.Wilkes.

were contemporaries of Newton were engrossed in experiments that would undermine the foundations of alchemy and provide the first real evidence to support Democritus's atomic theory of matter. The first breakthroughs in this area would come through the study of gases.

THE BEGINNING OF THE END OF ALCHEMY: BOYLE'S LAW

The brilliant Irish chemist Robert Boyle (1627–1691) was one such researcher. In one experiment, using a vacuum pump designed by his assistant Robert Hooke, Boyle removed all of the air in a closed chamber and proved that air was necessary for the transmission of sound and for candle flames to burn.

In his most famous experiment, Boyle sealed the opening of the shorter leg of a J-shaped glass tube and then poured mercury into the longer leg. This trapped the air in the short leg of the tube between

The chemist Robert Boyle is depicted in this 1670 engraving by J. Chapman. Note the chemistry equipment that appears below his portrait image.

the seal and the mercury. He continued to pour until the mercury in both the long and the short legs of the tube was at the same level. Then Boyle poured thirty more inches of mercury into the long end of the tube, in effect doubling the atmospheric pressure. The additional mercury compressed the air in the short leg of the tube to half its original volume. Thus Boyle had doubled the pressure on the trapped air and halved its volume.

Boyle's Law, as it is now known, proved that gas pressure and volume are inversely related. Decrease the volume of a gas and you increase its pressure, and vice versa. What was significant about this discovery was that this is the way a gas would behave if it were composed of a mass of freely moving particles, with empty spaces between those particles that allowed the gas to compress or expand. In other words, the volume of a gas would be affected by an increase or decrease in pressure if that gas were composed of atoms. The scientific observations behind Boyle's Law clearly supported the atomic theory of matter.

Joseph Priestley's microscope is pictured here. It was built in 1767 by Benjamin Martin, an amateur scientist based in London. Priestley discovered oxygen, though he called it "dephlogisticated air."

THE DISCOVERY OF "PHLOGISTON"

Following in the footsteps of Boyle, many experimenters began to study the secrets of gases. In the process, they began to map out a scientific foundation for chemistry. Joseph Priestley (1733–1806) began his career as a clergyman in Leeds, England, but he became interested in scientific matters through his friendship with the American inventor and revolutionary Benjamin Franklin.

Priestley's most important work concerned his discovery of oxygen. He misinterpreted the results of his own experiment, however, because of his belief in the "phlogiston" theory. At the time, scientists were intensely curious about the process of combustion, which they believed would reveal much about the chemical nature of substances. Scientists observed that when something burned, most of its material disappeared, leaving only fragments or ashes. They concluded that, during combustion, materials released into the air a substance called phlogiston. A substance disintegrates into ashes when it burns because this mysterious phlogiston has been "freed" from that substance. A material like charcoal, which burned almost completely, was thought to be composed almost entirely of phlogiston.

Priestley heated mercury in air, using sunlight concentrated by a magnifying glass. The surface of the heated mercury gleamed and became coated with a red powder, which we now know to be mercury oxide. When Priestley removed this powder and heated it, it evaporated into two different gases. One was mercury vapor, which condensed quickly into droplets of pure liquid mercury. The other was a colorless gas, which Priestley found could rekindle a smoldering candlewick. He even inhaled quantities of this gas, and reported feeling "light and easy." Priestley had discovered oxygen, but at the time he called it "dephlogisticated air." He believed that the initial heating of the mercury had released all its phlogiston, so the heating of the resulting red powdery residue produced a purer kind of air entirely devoid of phlogiston.

The Weight of Air

The phlogiston theory was eventually debunked by the French chemist Antoine-Laurent Lavoisier (1743–1794), a man who knew and admired Priestley. It was only with great reluctance that Lavoisier challenged the man he thought so highly of.

Antoine-Laurent Lavoisier (in red jacket) shows colleagues his 1776 mercury heating experiment that revealed the composition of air. Lavoisier named the gases generated by this heating process oxygen and azote (nitrogen).

Lavoisier had a hunch that something was wrong with the phlogiston idea, and he believed that only precise and accurate measurement would reveal the truth. Lavoisier repeated Priestley's experiments, heating metals until they formed a "calx," a crust of what we know today is a metal oxide. For some reason, the calx always weighed more than the original, unheated metal. How could the metal be giving off phlogiston if it was gaining weight in the process?

Lavoisier theorized that the metal's weight gain must have come from combining with the air in the flask. He also realized that if some of the air in the flask combined with the metal, there should be a partial vacuum in the container. When he opened the flask, he was rewarded by a rush of air filling the vacuum that had been created. Lavoisier had demonstrated not that phlogiston flowed out of materials when they burned, but that a portion of the air was drawn into materials during combustion.

One thing still bothered Lavoisier. After measuring the vacuum created, he realized that only about one-fifth of the air in the flask was involved in the reaction. Why not all of it? After a discussion with Priestley, Lavoisier realized that air must consist of a combination of two gases, each with different properties, and that only one of them was involved in the reaction. He went on to isolate this gas and named it oxygen, rejecting Priestley's theory of "dephlogisticated air." The other four-fifths of air Lavoisier called azote, from the Greek word meaning "no-life." Today, we call this gas nitrogen.

Lavoisier's work was revolutionary. In 1787, he published the first modern chemistry textbook. In this book, Lavoisier used Boyle's definition of an element as a substance that could not be broken down into simpler substances. He carefully described the qualities of the known elements and devised a set of symbols for them and a method for describing chemical reactions. Often regarded as the father of modern chemistry, Lavoisier came to an unpleasant end. During the French Revolution, he fell afoul of the radicals and died at the guillotine in 1794.

THE CHEMICAL REVOLUTION AND THE FRENCH REVOLUTION

At the very same time that Antoine-Laurent Lavoisier was revolutionizing the science of chemistry, another revolution was raging—the French Revolution (1789–1799).

Initially, it seemed that the overthrow of the French monarchy, the raising up of an egalitarian democracy, and the rejection of a superstition-riddled state religion would provide a congenial environment for Lavoisier and other French chemists. After all, these men were laboring to upset thousands of years of scientific misapprehension and magical thinking. Indeed, Lavoisier was a liberal who sympathized with the revolution's ideals. He served in an official capacity to help usher in political, economic, and social reforms. In particular, he advised the new government on matters of finance, was a member of a Commission for the Establishment of the Metric System, and was appointed Secretary of the Treasury in 1791.

Yet the revolutionaries ultimately turned against Lavoisier for his involvement during the pre-Revolutionary years with the Ferme Generale, a private company that collected taxes for the King. Ferme Generale tax collectors were often—and justifiably—accused of corruption, self-enrichment, and extravagant living. Lavoisier was guillotined in November 1794.

IDENTIFYING AND NAMING OXYGEN AND HYDROGEN

The theory of phlogiston was debunked definitively by a contemporary of Lavoisier, the eccentric English scientist Henry Cavendish (1731–1810). He conducted an experiment in which he added acid to metal, expecting that phlogiston would be produced by the reaction. This phlogiston would accumulate in a glass tube already filled with "dephlogisticated air," that is, oxygen. If a flame inserted into the tube continued to burn, it would "prove" the presence of phlogiston. The gas produced by the reaction was not phlogiston, but hydrogen. Cavendish noticed that droplets of liquid formed on the inner walls of the vessel in the presence of the flame. This condensation was water.

Lavoisier was ecstatic when he heard about Cavendish's results. He repeated the experiment and announced to the world that water was a compound— a material made up of two gases chemically combined. One gas, he knew, was oxygen. He named the other gas "hydrogen," from the Greek word for "water-producer." Each water molecule is made up of two hydrogen atoms and one oxygen atom. Lavoisier announced that water was an oxide of hydrogen, not one of Aristotle's fundamental "elements." Thus began the era of modern chemistry.

DISCOVERING CHEMICAL LAWS AND PROPERTIES

Chapter 3

E ven though Lavoisier's textbook had named the known elements and compounds, chemistry was still in its infancy. Lavoisier had incorrectly listed heat and light among the elements. And of the other elements he listed, a number were later discovered to be compounds. This problem plagued early chemists, who did not have the techniques to decompose all the existing compounds into their constituent elements or to isolate pure elements.

How could chemists identify and determine the nature of compounds, and upon what scientific principles were the particles that made up these compounds combining with one another? Several

Dessiné d'après le Portrait d'Albuerne et Gravé par Ambroise Tardieu.

LOUIS PROUST
(Chimiste),
membre de l'Académie des Sciences.
Né à .... (Dépt ......) le .... y ....

basic ideas were known and generally accepted by the scientific community. One such idea was the law of conservation of total mass, demonstrated by Lavoisier in his experiments with oxygen in 1798. The total mass of reactants in any chemical process was always equal to the total mass of the products of the chemical reaction. That is, mass, or matter, cannot be created or destroyed during a chemical reaction, though it can be transformed into a different kind of matter or substance.

THE LAW OF DEFINITE PROPORTIONS

Another general principle of the emerging field of chemistry was first demonstrated by Joseph Louis Proust (1754–1826). In 1799, Proust showed that no matter what processes were used to produce copper carbonate, the compound always contained the exact same proportion by weight of the elements copper, carbon, and oxygen. From this and other

Joseph Louis Proust, the developer of the law of definite proportions, appears in this eighteenth-century engraving. He was born in France but spent most of his life in Madrid, Spain, where he was the director of the Royal Laboratory.

experiments, Proust proved the law of definite proportions. This law states that the proportions of
elements in a specific compound do not vary. As
both Priestley and Lavoisier had discovered, one
unit volume of oxygen always combines with two units
volume of hydrogen to form water. That was true of
all chemical reactions, but it had become apparent
through the study of gases.

These laws seemed to suggest an underlying
reality of discrete particles—atoms—combining in
definite and fixed ways. Would scientists someday be
able to accurately describe that underlying reality?

PIONEERING THE IDEA OF ATOMIC WEIGHT

John Dalton (1766–1844) was an English Quaker
schoolteacher and chemist who tackled this problem. Dalton had experimented with gases and the
way they mixed easily with one another. He believed
that this could only happen if the gases were made
up of tiny individual particles with lots of empty
space between them. Dalton revived Democritus's
name for these particles—atoms. And he came to

believe that all matter, not just gases, was composed of atoms. He thought of atoms as solid, indestructible spheres that had no internal structure. He believed that the atoms of different substances could only be distinguished by their different masses or weights.

In his experiments, Dalton found that different compounds could result when the proportions— by weight—of the same constituent elements were altered. For example, he noticed that when he mixed three parts of carbon with four parts of oxygen, carbon monoxide always formed. But if he mixed three parts carbon with eight parts oxygen, the result was carbon dioxide. He reasoned, correctly, that a molecule of carbon monoxide is composed of one atom each of carbon and oxygen, and a molecule of carbon dioxide contains one atom of carbon and two atoms of oxygen.

These results confirmed the law of definite proportions. In 1803, Dalton came up with his own law, the law of multiple proportions, which stated that the same elements can combine in different ways to form different compounds. His experiments also demonstrated that there can be more than one atom of an element in a compound.

Dalton tried to determine the relative weight of each element in compounds. He found, for example,

ELEMENTS

Element	Wt.	Element	Wt.
Hydrogen.	1	Strontian	46
Azote	5	Barytes	68
Carbon	54	Iron	50
Oxygen	7	Zinc	56
Phosphorus	9	Copper	56
Sulphur	13	Lead	90
Magnesia	20	Silver	190
Lime	24	Gold	190
Soda	28	Platina	190
Potash	42	Mercury	167

that 1 gram of hydrogen always combines with exactly 8 grams of oxygen to form water. From this, he determined each element's "equivalent weight," that is, its weight in relation to other elements. Dalton continued to calculate the relative weights of other elements, and he was the first to work out a system of atomic weights for the known elements.

Dalton published his findings in favor of the atomic theory in a book entitled *A New System of Chemical Philosophy* in 1808. The book revolutionized the science of chemistry. Dalton's views put chemistry on a sound scientific footing, but he was not right about everything. For example, atoms are not solid, indestructible spheres lacking internal structure. Dalton also stubbornly believed that in a free or uncombined state, elements exist only as single atoms. In his view, only compounds could contain more than one atom of an element. Many of his atomic weights were wrong because he believed that like atoms would repel each other and could not combine. But other scientists were not so sure. New experimental techniques using electricity would seriously challenge Dalton's idea.

This 1806–1807 copy of John Dalton's table of elements is housed in the Science Museum in London.

ELECTROLYSIS PROVIDES GREATER CLARITY

In 1800, the Italian scientist Alessandro Volta invented the battery and produced the first electric current. Within months of this discovery, the English chemist William Nicholson used an electric current to separate the elements comprising a compound, a process called electrolysis by the English physicist Michael Faraday. It was now possible to break apart many compounds and precisely measure the relative weights of the elements that composed them.

In 1808, the French chemist Joseph Gay-Lussac (1778–1850) used electrolysis to determine the exact volume of hydrogen and the exact volume of oxygen that combined to form water, rather than trying to measure the weights of the two elements. He found that oxygen was able to combine with precisely twice its own volume of hydrogen. Based on this finding,

Joseph Gay-Lussac is depicted working in his laboratory in this nineteenth-century illustration. He was the first to hypothesize that a water molecule was composed of two hydrogen atoms and one oxygen atom.

EDITION
DE LA CHOCOLATERIE D'AIGUEBELLE

LES HÉROS DU TRAVAIL

GAY-LUSSAC

Gay-Lussac hypothesized that a water molecule consists of one atom of oxygen and two atoms of hydrogen. If water contained two atoms of hydrogen rather than one, its weight relative to oxygen was only one half of Dalton's value. Or, to put it another way, if the atomic weight of hydrogen were set at 1, the atomic weight of oxygen had to be 16, not 8. Dalton insisted that Gay-Lussac must have made a mistake in his experiment, but Gay-Lussac's work clarified and corrected a lot of inconsistencies associated with the atomic weights of the elements at this time.

DISTINGUISHING ATOMS FROM MOLECULES

In 1811, after studying the experiments of Gay-Lussac, the Italian chemist Amedeo Avogadro (1776–1856) put forward the idea that under identical conditions of temperature and pressure, all gases of equal volume contain an equal number of particles. This is

This illustration depicts two hydrogen atoms covalently bonded to an oxygen atom, forming a water molecule.

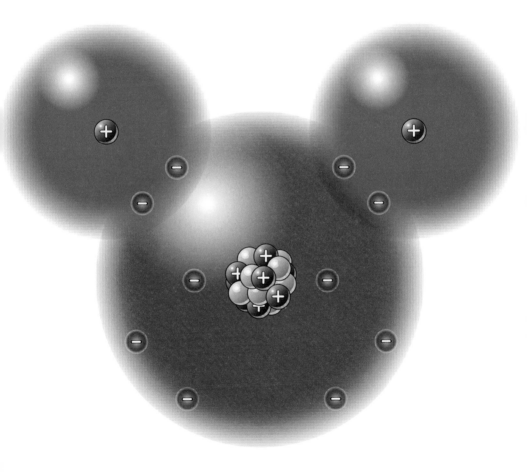

now known as Avogadro's Law. If the electrolysis of water yields twice the volume of hydrogen as oxygen, water must contain twice as many hydrogen particles as oxygen particles. So the formula for water could not be HO, as Dalton believed, but had to be H_2O (two atoms of hydrogen to one of oxygen).

Avogadro also experimented with hydrogen chloride (HCl). He combined 1 liter (34 ounces) each of hydrogen gas and chlorine gas. He expected to get ½ liter (17 oz.) of hydrogen chloride. Avogadro reasoned that if both hydrogen and chlorine exist as single atoms, once the atoms pair off, only half as many compound atoms are left. Avogadro was amazed when his experiment yielded a full liter (34 oz.) of hydrogen chloride. How was this possible?

After pondering this question, Avogadro suggested that if each gas particle contained two atoms of that gas, the problem was solved. One particle of hydrogen with two atoms, plus one particle of chlorine with two atoms, equal two particles of hydrogen chloride, each containing two atoms. Avogadro concluded that gaseous elements exist in diatomic form—as particles containing two atoms each— which refuted Dalton's "one-atom element" theory.

Avogadro was the first to distinguish between atoms and what he named "molecules" (a group of at least two atoms held together by chemical bonds). He was also the first to clear up the confusion between atomic and molecular weights.

THE ORIGINS OF THE PERIODIC TABLE

By the 1820s, experiments in chemistry were revealing new elements at an amazing rate. The Swedish chemist Jöns Jakob Berzelius (1779–1848) conducted thousands of experiments on compounds to determine the exact weight ratio between their constituent elements. He is credited with the discovery of the elements cerium, selenium, silicon, and thorium.

Berzelius prepared an extensive table of elements with accurate atomic weights, using a system of abbreviations based on the Latin names for the elements. This is why potassium is represented by the letter K, from the Latin *kalium*, and why gold is represented by Au, from the Latin *aurum*.

By 1860, just over sixty elements had been identified, and their relative atomic weights were known. A great deal was also known about their chemical properties. In 1869, Dmitri Ivanovich Mendeleev (1837–1907), a chemistry professor at the University of St. Petersburg in Russia, was preparing a chemistry

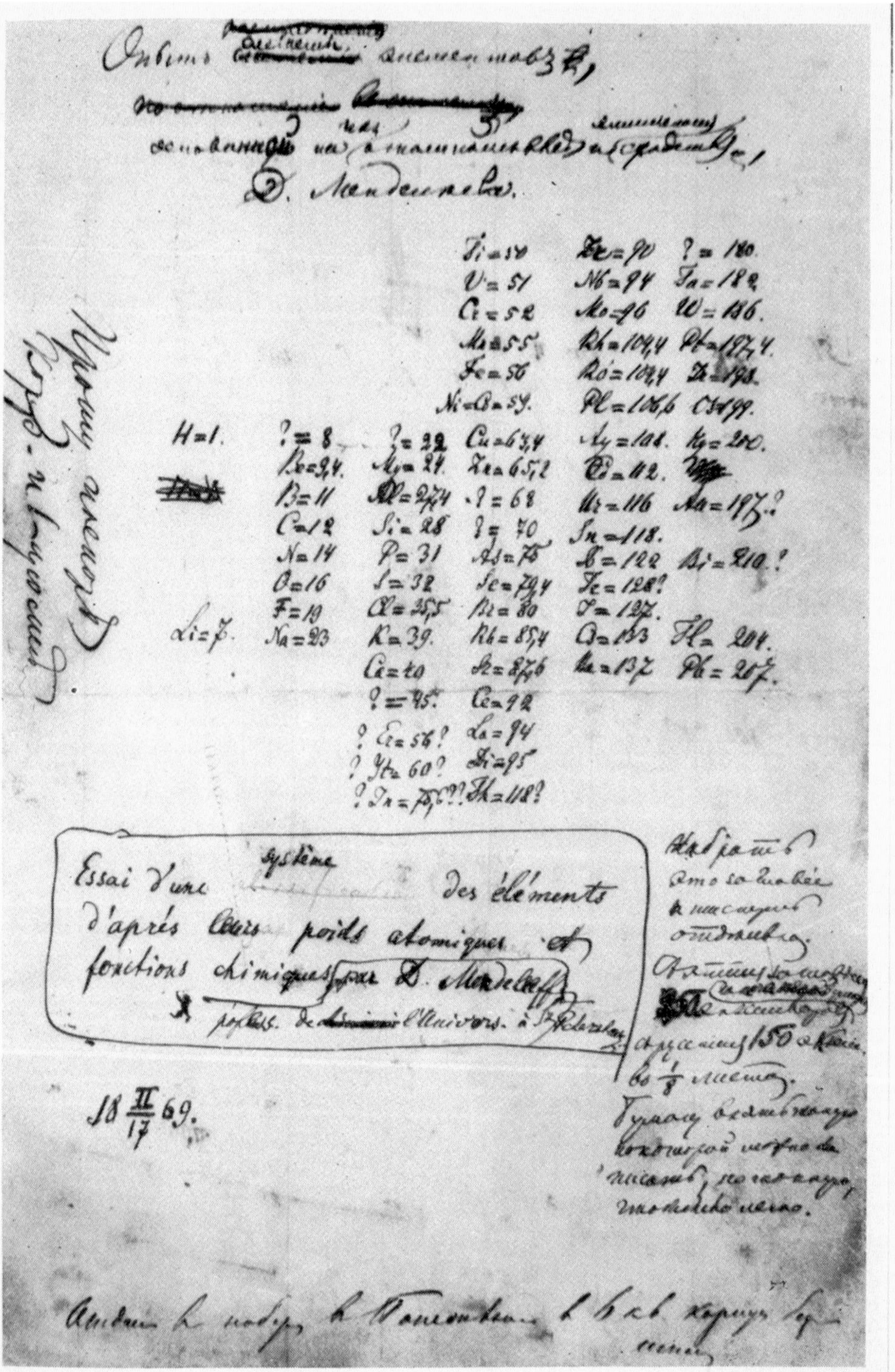

Д. Менделеева.

			Ti=50	Zr=90	?=180.
			V=51	Nb=94	Ta=182
			Cr=52	Mo=96	W=186.
			Mn=55	Rh=104,4	Pt=197,4.
			Fe=56	Ru=104,4	Ir=198.
			Ni=Co=59.	Pd=106,6	Os=199.
H=1.	?=8	?=22	Cu=63,4	Ag=108.	Hg=200.
	Be=9,4.	Mg=24.	Zn=65,2	Cd=112.	
	B=11	Al=27,4	?=68	Ur=116	Au=197?
	C=12	Si=28	?=70	Sn=118.	
	N=14	P=31	As=75	Sb=122	Bi=210?
	O=16	S=32	Se=79,4	Te=128?	
	F=19	Cl=35,5	Br=80	J=127.	
Li=7.	Na=23	K=39.	Rb=85,4	Cs=133	Tl=204.
		Ca=40	Sr=87,6	Ba=137	Pb=207.
		?=45.	Ce=92		
		?Er=56?	La=94		
		?Yt=60?	Di=95		
		?In=75,6??	Th=118?		

Essai d'une système des éléments d'après leurs poids atomiques et fonctions chimiques par D. Mendeleeff

18 II/17 69.

textbook for his students. He felt the need to put all the known elements into some kind of order. He began this monumental task by gathering every bit of information he could find about each element. He then studied and analyzed these properties looking for similarities.

Mendeleev wrote each element on a card. He tacked each card up on the wall. For the better part of a year, he studied the cards, arranging them in various rows and columns, based on what he knew about the elements' properties, searching for a logical order. At some point, Mendeleev arranged the cards in an order that struck him as meaningful. Hydrogen, as the lightest element, had been given first place in the upper left of his arrangement. Beneath hydrogen and running across the second row, Mendeleev had arrayed the cards for seven elements, from lithium to fluorine, in order of increasing atomic weight. In row three, he had placed the next seven elements, from sodium to chlorine, again in order of increasing atomic weight. A pattern began to make itself evident.

This is an 1869 manuscript page containing notes relating to Dmitri Ivanovich Mendeleev's first periodic system of elements, which grouped the known elements according to their atomic structure and chemical properties.

THE EVER-EXPANDING PERIODIC TABLE

Many people may look at the familiar periodic table that hangs in every chemistry classroom worldwide and assume that the chart is complete, finished, closed. Yet the periodic table continues to expand and incorporate newly discovered elements.

Antoine-Laurent Lavoisier was the first scientist to publish a list of the known elements in 1789. At that time, there were only thirty-three such elements. By 1869, when Dmitri Mendeleev and Julius Lothar Meyer each brought out their periodic tables independently of each other, there were over sixty identified elements.

Today, the periodic table contains 118 chemical elements whose discoveries have been confirmed. Ninety-four of these are naturally occurring, while twenty-four of them are synthetic, having being produced artificially in labs and usually only existing for milliseconds. Some isotopes of elements that were first discovered synthetically in the lab, like plutonium-94 and neptunium-43, -61, and -93, have since been found to exist in very small amounts in nature during the process of radioactive decay. The last naturally occurring element to be discovered was francium in 1939.

Since 1999, six elements have been discovered and confirmed but not yet formally named. They have received temporary names, which are the Latin words for their atomic number (ununhexium for 116, ununseptium for 117, ununoctium for 118, etc.). The most recent element to be discovered was ununseptium in 2009. It was discovered by the Joint Institute for Nuclear Research and the Lawrence Livermore National Laboratory. At this point, it is thought to be the heaviest member of the halogen family, which also includes fluorine, chlorine, bromine, iodine, and astatine.

Mendeleev had arranged all the known elements in order of increasing atomic weight. By doing so, he discovered families of elements with similar chemical properties. Other patterns revealed themselves as well, such as groupings of metals and nonmetals at opposite sides of the periodic table. In order to fit elements with similar properties into their proper columns, however, Mendeleev had to leave gaps in his table. He felt sure that these gaps would be filled by elements yet to be discovered, and he even predicted what chemical properties those elements would have. By 1875, chemists had discovered three new elements predicted by Mendeleev, and his reputation as the greatest chemist of his time was assured.

ATOMIC RAYS, PARTICLES, AND RADIATION

Chapter

4

I n the 1870s, the English chemist William Crookes (1832–1919), investigating the effects of gas pressure on the flow of electric current, decided that he needed a sealed glass tube with a better vacuum in it than had ever been achieved before. Crookes tube, as it came to be called, was an early precursor of the cathode ray tubes found in television sets.

An early cathode ray tube appears in this photograph. William Crookes used it in the late nineteenth century to prove that cathode rays traveled in straight lines, cast shadows, heated objects, and could be deflected by a magnet.

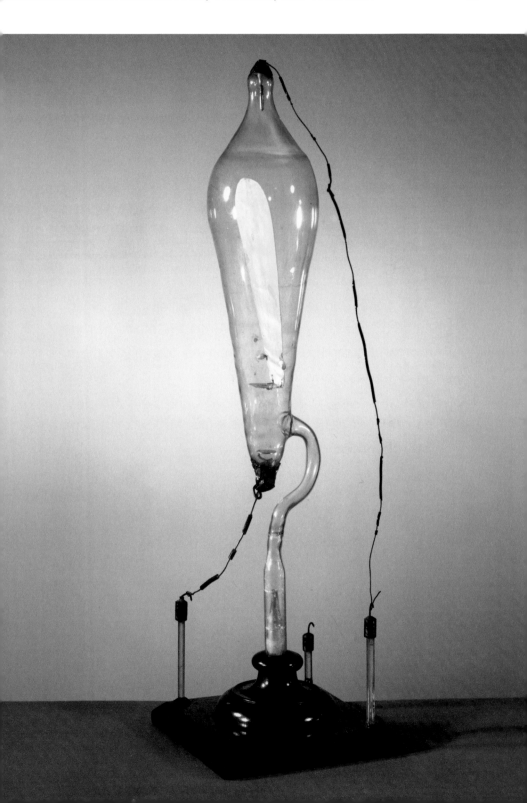

The device consisted of a sealed glass tube with two metal wires inside it. When the wires were connected to a battery and an electric current was passed through the tube, the negatively charged wire—the cathode—gave off radiation that made the tube fluoresce, or glow. When Crookes placed a small piece of metal in front of the cathode, a shadow was cast on the glass. This indicated that the radiation was flowing in a straight line. These mysterious emissions were dubbed "cathode rays."

Crookes pioneered the construction and use of vacuum tubes. He also discovered the element thallium and was the first person to identify helium. Crookes was one of the first scientists to investigate plasmas, and he developed one of the first instruments designed to measure radioactivity (the "spinthariscope").

INVESTIGATING CATHODE RAYS, DISCOVERING ELECTRONS

Scientists debated the nature of cathode rays. The rays could cast a shadow, so were they visible light? That is, were they waves? Others scientists were sure that they were charged particles, as Crookes himself believed, because they emerged from the negatively charged cathode.

Heinrich Hertz, the discoverer of radio waves, believed that cathode rays were waves. When he passed cathode rays between two electrically charged metal plates, the rays were not seen to deviate from their straight path. Since particles would have been deflected by the electromagnetic field surrounding the charged plates, Hertz believed that this experiment proved that the rays were waves. But he had not factored in the speed of the rays, which were so fast that his apparatus would not have been able to detect any deflection.

In 1897, the English physicist Joseph John Thomson (1856–1940) repeated the experiment that Hertz had tried earlier. Thomson, a Cambridge University graduate and student of James Clerk Maxwell, the discoverer of the laws of electromagnetism, was director of the Cavendish Laboratory at Cambridge. He had earlier calculated the speed of cathode rays. Armed with this crucial knowledge and a Crookes tube that created a more perfect vacuum, Thomson shot an electric current past two sheets of charged metal, as Hertz had done. He observed a distinct curve in the rays' path as they sped through the electromagnetic field created by the charged metal

RAYS TO THE RESCUE

Both X-rays and gamma rays are forms of electromagnetic radiation. The two are distinguished from each other in that X-rays generally have a longer wave length (though the wavelengths of X-rays and gamma rays occasionally overlap) and the fact that X-rays are emitted by electrons outside the nucleus. Gamma rays are emitted by the nucleus.

X-rays can be "hard" or "soft." Soft X-rays have longer wavelengths and, unlike hard X-rays, cannot penetrate solid objects. Gamma rays have the smallest wavelength of any wave in the electromagnetic spectrum, yet they also have the most energy. They are so powerful that they can kill living cells and organisms. For this reason, they are often used to attack cancer cells and irradiate medical equipment and food, ridding them of harmful bacteria. X-rays are also used in the health sciences, mainly as a diagnostic and medical imaging tool. Yet due to the fact that both rays are radioactive, they pose a cancer risk to people exposed to them.

Because of their ability to penetrate solid objects, both X-rays and gamma rays are increasingly being used for security purposes, particularly in luggage and cargo scanners.

strips. This was convincing evidence that cathode rays were particles. At the suggestion of the physicist G. J. Stoney, Thomson called these particles "electrons," each carrying the smallest, indivisible quantity of electric charge.

Revising Atomic Theory

Thomson's most revolutionary finding, however, came when he analyzed the degree of curvature in the electron's path as it passed through the electromagnetic field. Knowing the strength of the field, the speed of the particle, and its amount of deflection, he was able to calculate the mass of a single electron. According to Thomson, that mass was only 1/1,837 that of the hydrogen atom. Thomson had discovered a particle that was smaller than the atom, which was supposedly the smallest indivisible particle that existed.

The new discovery required a revised theory of what the atom was. It was certainly not the solid, featureless ball imagined by Dalton. Thomson conceived of the atom as a sphere of some permeable or spongy material with a positive charge. Embedded within this sphere, like blueberries in a muffin or

This is an X-ray photograph taken by Wilhelm Roentgen of his wife's hand in December 1895. Because X-rays can pass through matter, they are now used to image and diagnose internal medical conditions and for security purposes, such as scans of travelers, luggage, and cargo.

raisins in oatmeal, were the negatively charged electrons. Thomson believed that electrons were always arranged in a definite way unique to each element.

The Discovery of X-Rays and Radioactivity

In 1895, the German physicist Wilhelm Roentgen discovered that the electric current running through a Crookes tube produced powerful rays that could expose photographic film. This was true even if the film were wrapped in a

material that prevented the penetration of light. He called these rays "X-rays."

The French physicist Antoine Henri Becquerel (1852–1908) became interested in reproducing these X-rays. He observed that a compound of the heavy element uranium also emitted some kind of radiation that could expose photographic film. He had not found X-rays, but a completely new kind of energy that seemed to be coming from the heart of a solid substance. Marie Curie had named these emissions "radioactivity."

ALPHA, BETA, AND GAMMA RAYS

Back at the Cavendish Laboratory in Cambridge, the discovery of X-rays and radioactivity fascinated Joseph John Thomson and his bright young assistant, the New Zealander Ernest Rutherford (1871–1937). Thomson gave Rutherford the task of investigating the nature of this new radiation.

Ernest Rutherford sits in his Cambridge, England, laboratory with his machine designed to count alpha particles. Rutherford, working with Hans Wilhelm Geiger (for whom the Geiger counter is named), discovered the alpha, beta, and gamma rays of radiation.

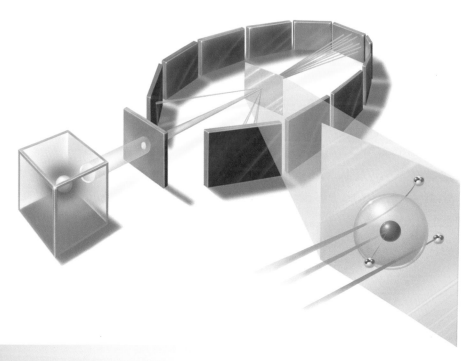

Here is Rutherford's particle scattering experiment. Radium emits alpha particles that pierce a sheet of gold foil. Some particles pass through the sheet without being deflected, others are deflected at a tiny angle, and a few are reflected at a large angle.

Rutherford began by subjecting uranium emissions to a powerful magnetic field. Through this experiment, he discovered that there were really three different kinds of rays. The path of one ray was bent by the magnet and was attracted to a negatively charged electric terminal. This suggested that the ray was positively charged and was actually a particle. Rutherford called these positively charged rays "alpha rays." He eventually realized that alpha rays were particles, and today we know them to be the nuclei of helium atoms, containing two protons and two neutrons.

Another ray was also bent by the magnet and was attracted to a positively charged electrode. Rutherford called these rays "beta rays," and they had properties remarkably like electrons, which is what they were.

The third type of ray could not be bent by the magnet. This ray was the strongest and most penetrating, much like an X-ray, and was named the "gamma ray." This proved to be a true wave of electromagnetic energy. Rutherford was the first to suggest that these rays and particles were the result of the decay of atoms, which transformed themselves into other elements as they released these particles.

BUILDING A BETTER ATOMIC MODEL

Chapter 5

When Ernest Rutherford realized that the alpha ray was really some kind of massive particle, he decided to use this particle as a kind of bullet to explore the inner structure of the atom. From 1906 to 1909, Rutherford, working with his assistants Ernest Marsden and Hans Geiger, used the alpha particles from a sample of radioactive material to bombard very thin sheets of metal foil. On the other side of the metal foil was a photographic plate to record the passage of any alpha particles that passed through the metal.

If J. J. Thomson's model of the atom was correct, the expectation was that almost all of the heavy alpha particles would travel straight through the metal foil, pushing aside the tiny electrons or being only slightly deflected by their negative charge. When Rutherford's assistants performed the experiment, however, they thought that they had made a mistake. Most of the alpha particles went straight through the metal foil, but a very few were deflected and scattered in odd directions. A few particles were even deflected at angles greater than 90 degrees, back toward the source of radiation.

Exploring and Mapping the Nuclear Atom

Rutherford suggested that some electrical force powerful enough to deflect the huge particles had to be involved. This force had to be concentrated within an extremely small space because only those few alpha particles that came near this force were diverted by it. Rutherford believed that this scattering backward must be the result of a single collision. In order to have a deflection of that magnitude, the majority of the mass of the atom must be concentrated in a very small nucleus carrying a charge. And because most of the alpha particles had passed right through the metal foil, Rutherford proposed that an atom is, in fact, mostly empty space. He theorized that the atom had an extremely dense core—or

nucleus—but was surrounded by empty space and electrons.

With this theory, Rutherford had introduced the modern idea of the nuclear atom. The notion that electrons surround or "orbit" the nucleus, like a miniature solar system, was a powerful analogy, and Rutherford's model came to be known as the planetary model of the atom. The electrons were bound to the nucleus by the attraction of their opposite electric charges, the way that gravity binds the planets to the sun.

In later experiments that involved bombarding the atoms of gases with alpha particles, Rutherford was able to demonstrate the presence of distinct positively charged particles within the nucleus. Rutherford called these positively charged nuclear particles "protons." Rutherford also determined that the electrons were the only particles involved in chemical reactions, and that the composition of the nucleus was not altered in the process. When he bombarded nitrogen atoms with alpha particles, however, he was able to transmute nitrogen into oxygen by changing the number of protons in the

This is a time-exposed photograph of an animated model of a uranium-235 atom. The center represents the nucleus. The fine lines represent the electrons spinning around the nucleus.

nucleus. In so doing, Rutherford achieved the dream of the alchemists. He was awarded the Nobel Prize for his work in 1908.

ATOMIC NUMBER ANSWERS OLD QUESTIONS AND RAISES NEW ONES

Discovering and mapping the nuclear atom was a neat little trick, but there were still a number of unresolved questions. One such problem was the discrepancy between atomic weight and the atom's electric charge.

In 1913, British physicist Henry Moseley decided to bombard a number of different metals with electrons and measure the frequency of the X-rays the metals produced. He initially thought that the frequency of the X-rays increased when they were emitted by elements with greater atomic weight. But several discrepancies in his data made him realize that the X-ray

Henry Moseley is best known for identifying atomic number, the positive electric charge carried by protons in an atom's nucleus. With the help of the atomic number, he revised the periodic table, placing the elements in a more logical order.

frequency was increasing as the electric charge of the nucleus increased. Moseley called the units of positive electric charge in the nucleus the "atomic number," to distinguish them from atomic weight.

Now the workings of the electromagnetic force that held the atom together were becoming clearer. The positive electric charge in the nucleus was carried by the protons, and the greater the number of protons, the greater the electric charge. The number of positively charged protons in the nucleus of an atom in a normal state was matched by the same number of orbiting negatively charged electrons.

But there was still a problem. Why was there this discrepancy between atomic number and atomic weight? Why were atoms so much heavier than the number of protons their nucleus contained? The nucleus of the oxygen atom, for example, had an electric charge eight times the charge exerted on the hydrogen nucleus because it contained eight protons. But its atomic weight was sixteen times the weight of the hydrogen nucleus. What made up this extra mass? And if the nucleus of the atom was made up only of positively charged protons, why didn't the nucleus fly apart as a result of the repelling force of the interaction of particles of the same electric charge? What held the nucleus together? What other mysteries did the nucleus of the atom hold?

THE MISSING PIECE OF THE ATOMIC PUZZLE: THE NEUTRON

If you look at a modern periodic table, the atomic weights of the elements are at the bottom of each element's box. The atomic weight of chlorine, for example, is given as 35.453. But if atomic weights are supposed to be whole multiples of the weight of the hydrogen atom, how can an element have a fractional atomic weight like this? It turns out that this number is an average of the atomic weights of two different types of chlorine atoms found in a sample of the substance. For example, J. J. Thomson had discovered two forms of neon gas with different atomic weights (neon-20 and neon-22), but he could not account for the mass difference.

The English chemist Frederick Soddy (1877–1956), who had worked with Rutherford, coined the term "isotope" to describe these variations of the basic elements. Soddy studied the radioactive decay of the element thorium and noted that it transmuted itself into different versions of thorium, all with the same chemical properties but different atomic weights. Because their atomic numbers and chemical properties were identical, Soddy believed that

This detector was used by James Chadwick in his discovery of the neutron. Inside the detector, particles from a radioactive source hit a beryllium target. From the resulting nuclear reactions, neutrons were given off. These were detected by Chadwick when they dislodged protons from a piece of paraffin wax.

all of these variations should occupy the same place in the periodic table. In addition, because each isotope had the same number of protons in its nucleus, its electrical and chemical characteristics were the same, but its mass differed from other isotopes. This discrepancy disturbed scientists and threatened to invalidate the elegant organization of Mendeleev's periodic table. How could a single element have different atomic weights?

The answer did not begin to emerge until the 1930s, with the experiments of the English physicist James Chadwick (1891–1974), another student of Ernest Rutherford's. After the work of Thomson and Rutherford and the discoveries of the electron and the proton, many scientists suspected that the "extra" mass in the atomic nucleus was caused by the presence of an as yet undiscovered particle with about the same mass as the proton. The problem was that this particle appeared to lack either a positive or negative electric charge. It was electrically neutral and would not be influenced or deflected from its path by an electric or magnetic field. If such a particle existed, it could not be detected by the usual means.

Chadwick solved this problem in 1932, when he bombarded the metal beryllium with alpha particles. He placed a piece of paraffin on the opposite side of the beryllium sample. No radiation could be detected between the beryllium and the paraffin, but Chadwick was able to detect protons being ejected from the paraffin with great force. Here was evidence that an electrically neutral particle, massive enough to push protons around, was emanating from the beryllium. Chadwick called the particle a "neutron."

Now everything began to fit into place. Chadwick's discovery resolved the discrepancy between atomic weight and atomic number. The number of protons in an element always stayed the same. The number of protons determined the number of electrons bound to the atom in its normal state, and hence the atom's chemical properties. But the total mass of an atom was also determined by the number of neutrons in the nucleus. These neutrons added weight but no electric charge. An element might have different numbers of neutrons in its nucleus, and this determined which isotope it was. The nucleus of chlorine-35, for example, contained 17 protons and 18 neutrons, but chlorine-37 contained 17 protons and 20 neutrons.

Miniscule but Mighty: The Pion

An explanation for what held the nucleus together against the repelling force of the tightly packed protons was not long in coming. In 1935, the Japanese scientist Hideki Yukawa (1907–1981) proposed the existence of a nuclear force exerted by all protons and neutrons. It could only exert its effects over a very short range—the diameter of the nucleus—but it was a very powerful force that could overcome the electric repulsion of the protons and hold the nucleus together. The neutrons in the nucleus, exerting nuclear force but no electric charge, helped keep the whole structure together.

Hideki Yukawa won the Nobel Prize in Physics in 1949 for his work on theoretical physics and elementary particles, particularly his theory of the existence of a transfer particle known as the pi-meson.

Yukawa's theory was based on the idea that the nuclear force resided in a transfer particle, about one-tenth the mass of a proton or neutron, that rapidly shuttled back and forth between the larger nuclear particles, thereby binding them together. In 1947, the English physicist Cecil Frank Powell (1903–1969) detected such a particle, which was named a pi-meson, or pion. Yukawa's theory was proven, and he received the Nobel Prize in 1949. Since then, Yukawa's work has mostly been devoted to theoretical physics and the theory of elementary particles (particles without a substructure, meaning not made up of smaller particles).

SUBATOMIC PARTICLES IN SPACE

So-called dark matter is an unidentified, mysterious form of matter that is believed to account for 85–98 percent of the universe. Despite its superabundance, astrophysicists have been unable to identify or detect the matter. What they have been able to do is to measure the gravitational pull it seems to exert on regular matter. This is as close to a proof of its existence as they have at this point.

The prevailing theory now is that dark matter is actually undetectable subatomic particles. At the origins of the universe, when it was younger and smaller, dark matter particles may also have acted as their own antiparticles. This means that when two dark matter particles drew close, they would destroy each other in a matter/antimatter reaction that generated extreme releases of energy. Some of these dark matter particles may have collected together and, in their high-energy matter/antimatter reactions, formed the nucleus of dark stars.

No one is certain if dark stars ever really existed. If they did, they would have been anything but dark. In fact, they would have been the brightest bodies in the young universe, due to that high-energy reactive core of dark particles. The bulk of dark stars, however, are believed to be composed of normal matter. The dark matter nucleus of dark stars would burn out quickly, to be replaced by a new nucleus of normal matter. At this point, the more typical nuclear fusion process would begin, and the formerly dark star would become a normal star. It is possible that some stars shining in the sky today are former dark stars, with their subatomic dark matter nuclei burned out and replaced and reignited by ordinary matter.

An Improved but Still Flawed Model

The picture of the atom now seemed to be complete. Unlike Dalton's solid little ball, the atom had turned out to have a very complex structure of subatomic particles. The new model was an elegant one in which the atom functioned like a tiny solar system.

As many scientists soon began to realize, however, this, too, was a model that wouldn't quite work. Though the solar system model of the atom is useful and still taught today, it is not a complete picture. If the electrons were orbiting the nucleus of the atom, Maxwell's theory of electromagnetism required them to give off energy. All electrically charged particles that accelerated—that changed their speed or direction, as orbiting electrons had to do—had to give off energy. But if electrons gave off energy, they would have to slow down in the process. They would then lose momentum and spiral into the nucleus. The whole atomic structure would collapse. Yet this was not the case; as scientists observed, atomic structure was remarkably stable in normal circumstances. An accurate understanding of the atom, its processes and inner workings, remained elusive.

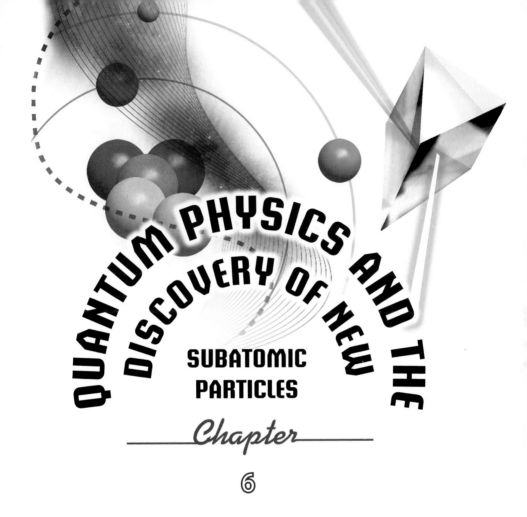

QUANTUM PHYSICS AND THE DISCOVERY OF NEW SUBATOMIC PARTICLES

Chapter

6

The problem of the stability of electron orbits in the Rutherford model of the atom found its solution thanks to the Danish physicist Niels Bohr (1885–1962). Bohr began to think about the atom in terms of some new ideas that had been developed by Max Planck (1858–1947) and Albert Einstein (1879–1955) at the very beginning of the twentieth century. Bohr would go on to work on the Manhattan Project, which led to the development of the first atomic bomb. He would also win a

Niels Bohr *(left)* confers with Max Planck. Both physicists were central to the development of quantum physics, and both were awarded the Nobel Prize in Physics.

Nobel Prize for his work on atomic structure and quantum mechanics.

QUANTUM PHYSICS STABILIZES THE ATOM

Planck, working at the University of Berlin, in Germany, was trying to solve an odd problem in the way objects radiated energy when they were heated. The frequency distribution of the radiated energy could not be explained by the laws of classical physics that conceived of light as made up of continuous waves. In 1900, unable to find a more acceptable explanation and in what he described as "an act of desperation," Planck announced his new quantum theory. The theory states that objects emit energy in tiny discrete packets or bundles, rather than as continuous waves. The size or amount of energy in the packet is related to the frequency detected when the wave-like qualities of energy are measured.

Planck called these tiny packets of energy "quanta." A single bundle of energy is called a "quantum." Planck suggested that objects emit and absorb energy only in whole quanta, never in fractional amounts of energy. In 1905, Albert Einstein interpreted the results of another experiment in a way that confirmed the quantum theory.

Bohr had worked under J. J. Thomson at Cambridge and Ernest Rutherford in Manchester, England, before returning to Copenhagen, Denmark, in 1916. Planck's theory of the quantum intrigued him, and he began to see a relationship between these little bundles of energy and the way electrons might behave within the atom. Bohr rejected Rutherford's model of the atom as a miniature solar system. He believed that electrons don't emit energy as they orbit the nucleus because they are not really orbiting in the sense that scientists had previously understood the term. It was more useful to think of these orbits as energy levels.

In a fixed orbit or energy level, the electron is in a stable state and emits no energy. But when an electron absorbs a quantum of energy, it jumps to a higher orbit or energy level, and is said to be in an excited state. When the electron jumps back to

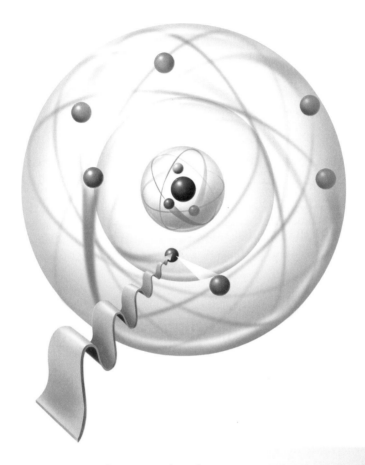

According to Bohr, electrons gravitate in circular orbits, each corresponding to a different energy level. For an electron to jump from one orbit to another, it must either receive or emit a certain amount of energy, called a quantum. This is known as the "quantum leap."

its original energy level, it emits energy in the form of a photon, which is a quanta or unit of energy in the range of visible light. The energy of the quantum emitted when the electron returns to its original state is exactly the same as the amount of energy the electron absorbed to jump to a higher orbit.

Bohr had created a model of the Rutherford atom that was stable. Unfortunately, the explanation forced scientists to abandon any "common sense" picture of what the atom might be like. The electron, rather than orbiting the nucleus like a little satellite, existed as a kind of ghost-like presence, a wave-particle, inside the atom.

Particles that Are Both There and Not There

One of the remaining problems facing scientists had to do with the strong nuclear force and the "exchange particles" that carried this force, the pi-mesons, that supposedly bound the protons and neutrons of the nucleus together. Such particles were somehow created in the nucleus and shuttled back and forth between the nuclear particles they held together. Hideki Yukawa had calculated that this particle had to be about 270 times as massive as an electron. But how could such a massive particle just appear from nowhere? Its existence violated the principle that neither matter nor energy could be created or destroyed.

ONGOING WORK ON ATOMIC STRUCTURE AND QUANTUM THEORY

The atom has not yet revealed all its mysteries. Indeed, with every question that is answered about the atom's structure, new ones pop up. Scientists may never finish exploring the micro-universe that is the atom. In 2010, the National Science Foundation (NSF) awarded Williams College professor Protik Majmuder a three-year, $285,000 grant to help fund his project entitled "Precise Atomic Structure Measurements and Tests of Fundamental Physics in Group IIIA Atoms." Majmuder's work involves extremely precise measurements of atomic structure with the help of semiconductor diode lasers. The NSF grant award states that:

In this project, carefully controlled lasers will be used to probe the detailed atomic structure of a class of heavy atoms, including thallium and indium, with unprecedented precision. Atoms, quintessential quantum mechanical objects, have long been used to confirm and test quantum theory. But in recent years, with advances in laser, optical, and

(Ongoing Work on Atomic Structure and Quantum Theory continued)

signal processing technology, extremely precise experiments on certain heavy atoms have yielded insights into physics more commonly associated with elementary particles and large accelerators. Such tests of fundamental particle physics in these "table-top" experiments can only occur through both precise experiments and also sophisticated quantum mechanical calculations of these many-electron systems. Experiments in this laboratory using atoms in both heated vapor cells and atomic beam apparatus will be completed to test the accuracy of this cutting-edge atomic theory.

The answer came from the work of the German physicist Werner Heisenberg (1901–1976). Heisenberg had studied the nature of the electron, and, in 1927, he set forth his uncertainty principle. The uncertainty principle states that you cannot simultaneously measure both the position and the momentum of an object with complete accuracy. With large objects, the inaccuracy was very small. But on the scale of subatomic particles, and the electron in particular, the inaccuracy was significant. This physical limit on obtaining precise information about the movement of subatomic particles indicated to Heisenberg that the world of the atom could not be explained in the same terms as the everyday world, and he abandoned any attempt to devise a visual model for what the atom was. The precise orbits of electrons could never be measured.

As a result of relationships Einstein had discovered, it was possible to substitute energy and time for position and momentum in Heisenberg's uncertainty formula. That is to say, at any exact point in time the energy (or mass, according to Einstein) of an object remains uncertain. If the time interval was small enough, so small in fact that it was impossible to measure, particles could come into being, violating the laws of conservation of mass and energy, as long as they disappeared again before they could be detected. Because such particles could not exist in real time in the real world, they were called "virtual particles."

As bizarre as the notion of virtual particles like mesons may seem, they are real, and in fact they have been detected. Within the atom in its normal state, they are undetectable. But if enough energy is added to the atom from an outside source, mesons can be created and can exist as independent particles without violating the laws of conservation of matter and energy. Bombarding atoms with enormous amounts of energy in particle accelerators has proven the key to the discovery of many new particles that would not otherwise reveal themselves.

Werner Heisenberg, shown here teaching in 1936, was a pioneer of quantum physics. He developed the uncertainty principle, which stated that the more precisely the position of a subatomic particle is measured, the less precisely its momentum is known.

QUARKS, GLUONS, AND OTHER FUNDAMENTAL PARTICLES AND ANTI-PARTICLES

By the mid-1960s, so many new particles had been discovered that physicists were forced to abandon the older model of the atom as composed only of such ordinary subatomic particles as protons, neutrons, and electrons. It no longer seemed that these particles were the most basic and fundamental components of the atom and of matter. Physicists began to suspect that even more basic forms of matter composed all subatomic particles.

In 1963, the American theoretical physicist Murray Gell-Mann proposed that all subatomic particles were themselves composed of even smaller particles, which he called "quarks." Gell-Mann stated that quarks were the truly fundamental building blocks of matter. As scientists built more powerful particle accelerators, they were able to discover evidence for the existence of quarks, confirming Gell-Mann's work. The quarks themselves can never be detected, but they quickly decay into other particles that can be detected. The discovery of these quarks was proof of what physicists now call the standard model of atomic structure.

In the standard model, all the more massive particles, like protons and neutrons, are made up of combinations of two or three quarks. Less massive particles like electrons, mesons, and neutrinos are not composed of quarks and are considered fundamental particles in their own right. They belong to a family of particles known as leptons. The various fundamental forces of nature that bind these particles together are all carried by exchange particles. The electromagnetic force is transmitted by the photon. The strong nuclear force is transmitted by the gluon, and the weak nuclear force, required to explain radioactive decay, is carried by particles known as W and Z bosons.

The quark structure of the carbon nucleus is illustrated here. The most common isotope, carbon-12, consists of six protons and six neutrons. These are represented as triplets of quarks surrounded by quantum clouds of gluons. The clouds of gluons hold the quarks together.

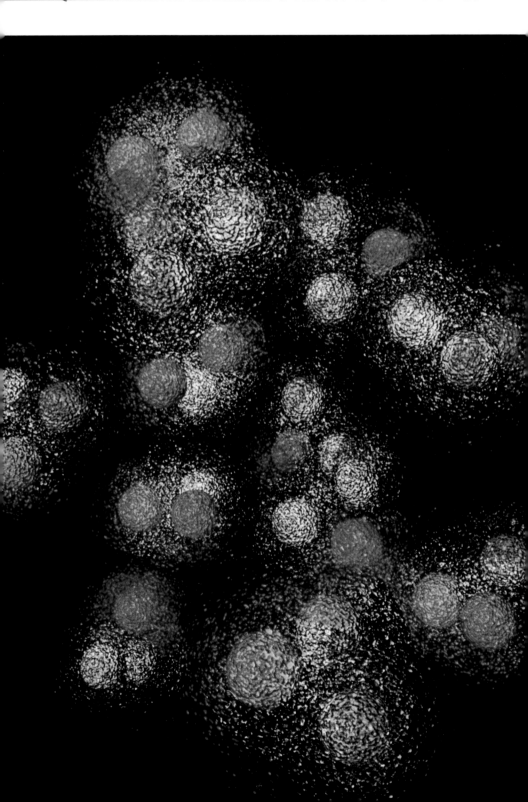

We have come a long way from the tiny, indivisible spheres of Democritus and the early atomists. We now know that the atom has a complex internal structure of subatomic particles, and that those particles obey laws of nature very different from those we are familiar with in our everyday experience. Our current model of the atom allows us to explain many things: how the fundamental elements differ from one another, how chemical combinations occur, why radioactive elements decay, how objects radiate energy, and how to build everything from televisions to lasers.

There is also much that we don't yet know. Can we ever describe the reality behind subatomic objects that sometimes behave like particles and sometimes like waves? Will we ever discover the relationship between the three forces that govern atomic behavior and the fourth force in the universe, gravity, thereby achieving the long sought after goal of a "theory of everything"? Will we find a deeper reality behind the quantum laws of probability that make electrons and other particles seem to live a ghostly, unreal existence? Are subatomic particles stable, or will protons decay in billions of years, bringing an end to the material world as we know it? And the greatest cosmic question of all, how did all of these particles come into existence in the first place? As far as we have come, there is certainly a lot more to discover for the next generation of young scientists.

5000 BCE The study and practice of alchemy originates in Egypt.

4000 BCE Egyptians heat combinations of sand, limestone, and soda (sodium carbonate) until the materials melt and turn into glass.

2000 BCE The Bronze Age begins when rocks containing copper and rocks containing tin are heated together. The combination of the two metals yields the metal alloy bronze.

1500 BCE The Hittites are credited with the discovery of iron.

600 BCE Thales of Miletus states that all material things are aspects of one fundamental substance—water. He suggests that the amount of water in a substance gave it its unique characteristics.

300 BCE Democritus says that matter is made up of solid atoms and empty space. Atoms were indivisible, the smallest pieces of substances that existed. They were not only solid, but they were invisible to the naked eye. Aristotle counters with his theory stating that there were four elements, and each of these elements was a combination of two of four opposites—hot and cold, and wet and dry.

1600s Robert Boyle develops Boyle's Law, which proved that gas pressure and volume are inversely related. This is the way a gas would behave if it were composed of a mass of freely moving particles, with empty spaces between those particles that allowed the gas to compress or expand. In other words, the volume of a gas would be affected by an increase or decrease in pressure if that gas were composed of atoms. The scientific observations behind Boyle's Law clearly supported the atomic theory of matter.

1700s Joseph Priestley discovers oxygen, but he calls it "dephlogisticated air." Antoine-Laurent Lavoisier will later identify and name both oxygen and nitrogen. Lavoisier also carefully describes the qualities of the known elements and devises a set of symbols for them and a method for describing chemical reactions. He and Henry Cavendish would identify hydrogen and discover that water was actually a compound of hydrogen and oxygen.

1799 Joseph Louis Proust proves the law of definite proportions. This law states that the
proportions of elements in a specific compound do not vary.

1800 William Nicholson uses an electric current to separate the elements comprising a
compound.

1803 John Dalton develops the law of multiple
proportions, which states that the same elements can combine in different ways to form
different compounds. His experiments also
demonstrate that there can be more than one
atom of an element in a compound. Dalton
is the first to work out a system of atomic
weights for the known elements.

1808 Joseph Gay-Lussac uses electrolysis to
determine the exact volume of hydrogen
and the exact volume of oxygen that combined to form water, rather than trying to
measure the weights of the two elements.
He finds that oxygen is able to combine
with precisely twice its own volume of
hydrogen. Based on this finding, Gay-
Lussac hypothesizes that a water molecule

consists of one atom of oxygen and two atoms of hydrogen.

1811 Amedeo Avogadro puts forward the idea that under identical conditions of temperature and pressure, all gases of equal volume contain an equal number of particles. This is now known as Avogadro's Law. Avogadro was the first to distinguish between atoms and what he named "molecules" (a group of at least two atoms held together by chemical bonds). He was also the first to clear up the confusion between atomic and molecular weights.

1820s Jöns Jakob Berzelius conducts thousands of experiments on compounds to determine the exact weight ratio between their constituent elements. He is credited with the discovery of the elements cerium, selenium, silicon, and thorium. Berzelius prepares an extensive table of elements with accurate atomic weights, using a system of abbreviations based on the Latin names for the elements.

1870s Dmitri Ivanovich Mendeleev develops the modern periodic table. William Crookes discovers cathode rays.

1895 Wilhelm Roentgen discovers X-rays. Antoine Henri Becquerel studies X-rays and discovers radioactivity. Ernest Rutherford soon discovers alpha, beta, and gamma rays. Rutherford is the first to suggest that these rays and particles are the result of the decay of atoms, which transform themselves into other elements as they release these particles.

1897 Joseph John Thomson identifies and names electrons. Thomson conceived of the atom as a sphere of some permeable or spongy material with a positive charge. Embedded within this sphere were the negatively charged electrons. Thomson believed that electrons were always arranged in a definite way unique to each element.

1900 Max Planck introduces quantum theory.

1909 Rutherford proposes that an atom is, in fact, mostly empty space, with an extremely dense core—or nucleus—surrounded by empty space and electrons. In later experiments, he identifies and names protons and determines that the electrons are the only particles involved in chemical reactions, and that the composition of the nucleus is not altered in chemical reactions.

1913 Henry Moseley calls the units of positive electric charge in the nucleus the "atomic number," to distinguish them from atomic weight.

1927 Werner Heisenberg introduces his uncertainty principle, which states, in part, that precise orbits of electrons can never be measured.

1932 James Chadwick identifies and names the neutron.

1939 Francium is the last naturally occurring element to be discovered.

1947 Cecil Frank Powell detects a subatomic transfer particle, which is named a pi-meson, or pion.

1963 Murray Gell-Mann proposes that all subatomic particles are themselves composed of even smaller particles, which he calls "quarks."

2009 The most recent element to be discovered is ununseptium, by the Joint Institute for Nuclear Research and the Lawrence Livermore National Laboratory. At this point it is thought to be the heaviest member of the halogen family, which also includes fluorine, chlorine, bromine, iodine, and astatine.

2010 The National Science Foundation funds the work of Williams College professor Protik Majmuder that will use carefully controlled lasers to probe the detailed atomic structure of a class of heavy atoms, including thallium and indium, with unprecedented precision.

alchemy An ancient practice in which people attempted to transform one element into another, especially lead into gold.

alpha particle The nucleus of a helium atom, containing two protons and two neutrons.

anti-particle Every particle has an anti-particle with the same mass but with an opposite electric charge. When a particle and its anti-particle come into contact, they annihilate each other.

atom The basic unit of an element, consisting of nuclear particles and electrons (and their constituent particles, such as quarks and carrier particles). Most of the atom is empty space.

atomic number The number of protons in an atom's nucleus.

atomic weight The total number of protons and neutrons in an atom's nucleus; also called atomic mass.

beta particle An electron; beta radiation is a high-speed stream of electrons.

cathode rays The stream of electrons emitted by the negative electrode in a vacuum tube (Crookes tube).

compound Two or more elements chemically bound together in a fixed proportion.

electrolysis A process in which an electric current is used to separate elements in a compound.

electron The negatively charged particle in an atom. Electrons are now known to have properties of both particles and waves, and clouds of electrons orbit the nucleus.

element In modern physics and chemistry, any substance that cannot be broken down into different substances by ordinary chemical means.

gamma rays A stream of high-energy photons emitted as radiation from an atom's nucleus.

gluon A particle that carries, or transmits, the strong force in the nucleus of an atom.

gravity The attractive force exerted by every object on other objects. The graviton is believed to be the particle that carries the force of gravity, but so far it has not been detected.

Heisenberg's uncertainty principle A principle guiding the quantum world, which states that it is impossible to measure simultaneously and accurately both the energy and time (or location and momentum) of subatomic particles.

ion An atom with an electric charge, usually caused by the removal or addition of outer electrons.

isotopes Atoms of the same element that have different numbers of neutrons in the nucleus and thus have different atomic weights.

mass The amount of matter an object contains, or the degree of an object's resistance to being disturbed (its inertia). Though not precisely accurate, weight is a term commonly substituted for mass.

meson A subatomic particle that is made up of two quarks; for example, a pion.

molecule The smallest unit of any compound in which two or more atoms are bound together. Bonded atoms can be of the same element (as in a molecule of any gas) or of different elements (as in water).

neutron A subatomic particle in the nucleus that has no charge and is made up of three quarks.

nuclear decay A process in which an atomic nucleus becomes less massive by splitting apart or giving off particles as radiation.

nucleus The central part of the atom that contains most of the atom's mass; consisting of protons and neutrons.

particle decay A process in which a fundamental particle transforms itself into a completely different fundamental particle.

periodic table A table of the elements organized by atomic number and atomic weight, as well as by similar chemical properties.

phlogiston A mysterious material believed by the alchemists to be associated with burning. When a substance burned, they believed phlogiston was freed from it. When heat caused a substance to solidify, they thought phlogiston had been added to it.

photon A particle of light; the carrier of the electromagnetic force.

positron The anti-particle of an electron. It is like an electron (with the same mass), but with a positive electric charge.

proton The positively charged particle in the atomic nucleus.

quantum In quantum theory, minute "packages" of light energy (plural: quanta).

quark The fundamental particle that makes up protons and neutrons.

radioactivity Spontaneous disintegration of an atom's nucleus to form a different nucleus, during which particles and energy are emitted.

standard model The current model of the atom that states that all atoms are made up of six quarks and six leptons, acted on by four forces that are carried by exchange particles.

strong force The force that holds the atomic nucleus together. Gluons transmit the strong force among the quarks that make up subatomic particles in the nucleus.

valence The ability of an element to combine with other elements through the electrons in its outer orbit. Valence determines the chemical properties of elements.

virtual particle A very short-lived particle that would violate the law of conservation of energy and mass if it could be detected.

X-rays Extremely energetic electromagnetic rays that easily penetrate most materials, except platinum and lead, and that expose photographic film.

American Association for the Advancement of Science (AAAS)

1200 New York Avenue NW
Washington, DC 20005
(202) 326-6400
Web site: http://www.aaas.org

A 150-year old international organization, this group works to promote and advance all fields of science by fostering education, enhancing communication, promoting science and its uses, and increasing public involvement.

American Chemical Society (ACS)

1155 Sixteenth Street, NW
Washington, DC 20036
(800) 227-5558 (U.S.)
(202) 872-4600 (Worldwide)
Web site: http://portal.acs.org

The ACS is a professional and scholarly organization of chemists that puts out dozens of publications, holds conferences, and promotes chemistry in general.

American Institute of Physics (AIP)

One Physics Ellipse
College Park, MD 20740-3843
(301) 209-3100
Web site: http://www.aip.org

The AIP is an organization dedicated to promoting advancements and education in the field of physics. It provides helpful information for scientists, students, and the general public.

Chemical Heritage Foundation

315 Chestnut Street

Philadelphia, PA 19106

(215) 925-2222

Web site: http://www.chemheritage.org

The Chemical Heritage Foundation is an independent nonprofit organization whose goal is to foster knowledge about chemistry and its contributions, including public outreach, a chemical library, and other efforts.

Chemical Institute of Canada (CIC)

130 Slater Street, Suite 550

Ottawa, ON K1P 6E2

Canada

(613) 232-6252

Toll-free: (888) 542-2242

Web site: http://www.chemistry.ca

The CIC is an umbrella group of three organizations—the Canadian Society for Chemistry, the Canadian Society for Chemical Engineering, and the Canadian Society for Chemical Technology.

Fermilab

P.O. Box 500

Batavia, IL 60510-5011

(630) 840-3000

Web site: http://www.fnal.gov

This well-known lab conducts basic research into all elements of particle physics and has the world's second highest energy particle accelerator in the world.

Institute of Physics (IOP)

76 Portland Place
London, England W1B 1NT
Tel.: 44 (9) 7470 4800
Web site: http://www.iop.org

The IOP is a leading professional organization working to promote developments in physics. Its Web site includes information about conferences, research, and other topics in the field.

International Union of Pure and Applied Chemistry (IUPAC)

P.O. Box 13757
Research Triangle Park, NC 27709-3757
(919) 485-8700
Web site: http://www.iupac.org

The IUPAC addresses issues related to chemistry. In particular, it creates the rules for naming elements and compounds.

International Union of Pure and Applied Physics (IUPAP)

American Physical Society
One Physics Ellipse
College Park, MD 20740-3844
(301) 209-3269
Web site: http://www.iupap.org

The IUPAP promotes cooperation between physicists around the world. In particular, it sets standards for the symbols, units, and names used in physics.

Massachusetts Institute of Technology (MIT)

Department of Chemistry

77 Massachusetts Avenue

Cambridge, MA 02139-4307

(617) 253-1803

Web site: http://web.mit.edu/chemistry/www/
index.html

MIT is one of the most respected and prestigious universities
in the world specializing in science and technology, with a well-
known chemistry department.

National Research Council Canada (NRCC)

1200 Montreal Road, Building M-55

Ottawa, ON K1A 0R6

Canada

(613) 993-9084

Web site: http://www.nrc-cnrc.gc.ca

The NRCC is a scientific research organization run by the
Canadian government since 1916.

National Science Foundation (NSF)

4201 Wilson Boulevard

Arlington, VA 22230

(703) 292-5111

Toll-free: (800) 877-8339

Web site: http://www.nsf.gov

The National Science Foundation provides up to 20 percent of
all federally distributed funds to support science research at col-
leges and universities nationwide.

National Youth Science Foundation (NYSF)
P.O. Box 3387
Charleston, WV 25333-3387
(304) 342-3326
Web site: http://www.nysf.com
The National Youth Science Foundation is a nonprofit organization that supports and operates youth science education programs, including the National Youth Science Camp in West Virginia.

The Science Club
4921 Preston-Fall City Road
Fall City, WA 98024
(425) 222-5066
The Science Club is a nonprofit organization dedicated to increasing curiosity about science through easy and fun experiments. All of the activities use common household materials and can be done at home.

Web Sites

Due to the changing nature of Internet links, Rosen Publishing has developed an online list of Web sites related to the subject of this book. This site is updated regularly. Please use this link to access the list:

http://www.rosenlinks.com/phys/atom

Aloian, Molly. *Atoms and Molecules*. New York, NY: Crabtree Publishing Company, 2008.

Balibar, Sebastien. *The Atom and the Apple: Twelve Tales from Contemporary Physics*. Princeton, NJ: Princeton University Press, 2008.

Dalai Lama. *The Universe in a Single Atom: The Convergence of Science and Spirituality*. New York, NY: Broadway, 2006.

Gray, Theodore. *The Elements: A Visual Exploration of Every Known Atom in the Universe*. New York, NY: Black Dog & Leventhal Publishers, 2009.

Graybill, George. *Atoms, Molecules, and Elements*. San Diego, CA: Classroom Complete Press, 2007.

Haken, Herrman, and Hans Christoph Wolf. *The Physics of Atoms and Quanta: Introduction to Experiments and Theory*. New York, NY: Springer, 2010.

Hassani, Sadri. *From Atoms to Galaxies: A Conceptual Physics Approach to Scientific Awareness*. Boca Raton, FL: CRC Press, 2010.

McMurray, John, and Robert C. Fay. *General Chemistry: Atoms First*. Upper Saddle River, NJ: Prentice Hall, 2009.

Newman, William R. *Atoms and Alchemy: Chymistry and the Experimental Origins of the Scientific*

Revolution. Chicago, IL: Chicago University Press, 2006.

Paulson, Steve. *Atoms and Eden: Conversations on Religion and Science*. New York, NY: Oxford University Press, 2010.

Sussman, Art. *Dr. Art's Guide to Science: Connecting Atoms, Galaxies, and Everything in Between*. San Francisco, CA: Jossey-Bass, 2006.

Zumdahl, Steven S., and Susan A. Zumdahl. *Chemistry: An Atoms First Approach*. Florence, KY: Brooks Cole, 2011.

Index

ABOUT THE AUTHORS

Margaret Christine Campbell is a writer living in Plainsboro, New Jersey.

Natalie Goldstein has written numerous books on scientific topics, including biodiversity, the environment, ecosystems, oceans, global warming and climate change, vaccines, viruses and diseases, and germ theory.

PHOTO CREDITS

Cover, p. 4 © www.istockphoto.com/DSGpro; pp. 6–7 © Kenneth Eward/Photo Researchers, Inc.; p. 10 Scala/Art Resource, NY; pp. 13, 21, 30, 42, 47, 52–53, 66–67 SSPL/Getty Images; p. 15 Imagno/Getty Images; p. 18 Hulton Archive/Getty Images; pp. 24–25 © Sheila Terry/Photo Researchers, Inc.; p. 34 SSPL/Science Museum/Art Resource, NY; p. 37 © Mary Evans Picture Library/The Image Works; p. 39 Dorling Kindersley/Getty Images; p. 54 © Topham/The Image Works; pp. 56, 79 © BSIP/Photo Researchers, Inc.; pp. 60, 76–77 © Science Source/Photo Researchers, Inc.; p. 63 © New York Public Library/Photo Researchers, Inc.; pp. 70–71 Keystone/Getty Images; pp. 84–85 © AIP/Photo Researchers, Inc.; p. 87 © ArSciMed/Photo Researchers, Inc.

Photo Researcher: Amy Feinberg